FIREFIGHTER'S TOOLS

ANDERS HANSON

Consulting Editor, Diane Craig, M.A./Reading Specialist

A Division of ABDO

ABDO
Publishing Company

D1088349

visit us at www.abdopublishing.com

Published by ABDO Publishing Company, a division of ABDO,
P.O. Box 398166, Minneapolis, Minnesota 55439. Copyright © 2014
by Abdo Consulting Group, Inc. International copyrights reserved in all
countries. No part of this book may be reproduced in any form without
written permission from the publisher. Super SandCastle™
is a trademark and logo of ABDO Publishing Company.

Printed in the United States of America,
North Mankato, Minnesota
102013
012014

 PRINTED ON RECYCLED PAPER

Editor: Liz Salzmann
Content Developer: Nancy Tuminelly
Photo Credits: Shutterstock

Library of Congress Cataloging-in-Publication Data

Hanson, Anders, 1980- author.
 Firefighter's tools / Anders Hanson ; consulting editor, Diane Craig, M.A.,
reading specialist.
   pages cm. -- (More professional tools)
 Audience: Ages 5 to 10.
 ISBN 978-1-62403-073-4
 1. Fire extinction--Equipment and supplies--Juvenile literature. 2. Fire
fighters--Juvenile literature. I. Craig, Diane, consultant. II. Title.
 TH9372.H345 2014
 628.9'25--dc23
                    2013022517

Super SandCastle™ books are created by a team of professional
educators, reading specialists, and content developers around five
essential components—phonemic awareness, phonics, vocabulary,
text comprehension, and fluency—to assist young readers as they
develop reading skills and strategies and increase their general
knowledge. All books are written, reviewed, and leveled for guided
reading, early reading intervention, and Accelerated Reader®
programs for use in shared, guided, and independent reading and
writing activities to support a balanced approach to literacy
instruction.

CONTENTS

MEET A FIREFIGHTER!

WHAT DOES A FIREFIGHTER DO?

A firefighter's job is to put out fires. When people see a **dangerous** fire, they call the firefighters!

WHY DO FIREFIGHTERS NEED TOOLS?

Some tools protect firefighters or help them get places quickly. Other tools help firefighters put out fires or rescue people.

FIREFIGHTER'S TOOLS

Turnout Gear

Fire Hose

Hydraulic Rescue Tool

Fire Engine

TURNOUT GEAR

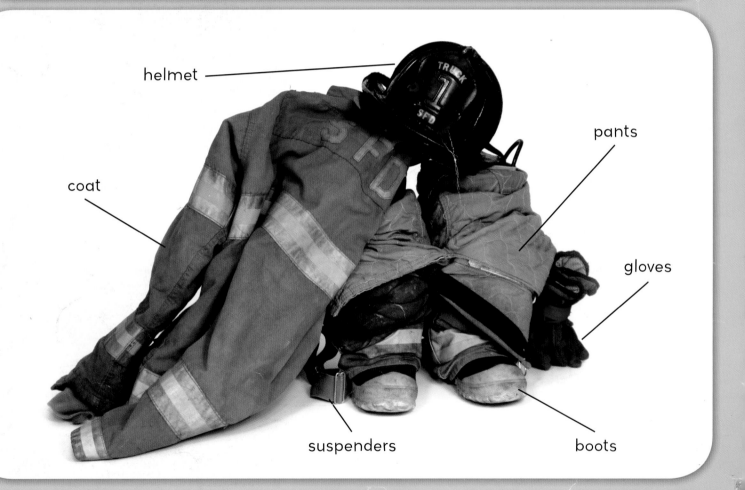

helmet

coat

pants

gloves

suspenders

boots

Turnout gear protects firefighters from heat.

Turnout gear is protective clothing. It is able to **withstand** 500-degree heat for five minutes or more.

Turnout gear includes a helmet, coat, gloves, pants, suspenders, and boots.

Fred is the Fire Chief. He directs the firefighters. Fred is wearing turnout gear.

James is on a tour of his local fire department.
He gets to dress up in turnout gear.

FIRE ENGINE

Fire engines carry firefighters and equipment to fires.

Fire engines have hoses and large ladders. Firefighters spray water through the hoses to put out fires. They use the ladders to reach tall fires and save people.

Fire engines also have **sirens**, horns, flashing lights, and two-way radios.

Fire engines are loaded with tools and **equipment.**
How many hoses can you find?

It takes a lot of water to put out large fires. Some fire engines hold up to 3,000 gallons (11,356 L) of water.

FIRE HOSE

hose

large nozzle

small nozzle

Fire hoses shoot water into fires.

A fire hose is a long tube with a **nozzle** at one end. Different types of nozzles can be **attached**. Each type of nozzle sprays water differently.

Most fire hoses are made of rubber and strong **fabric**.

Firefighters must be brave. Most people would run from the huge fire, but Tim walks toward it with his hose.

Some hoses are hard to control.
Teams of firefighters must hold them.

RESCUE TOOLS

Hydraulic pumps give these tools power.

Hydraulic rescue tools are great for helping people trapped in cars. They can cut and bend thick pieces of metal.

There are several types of hydraulic tools. Some are good for cutting. Others are better for spreading.

This tool has cutting jaws. They cut right though steel!

Sometimes car doors become stuck during an accident.
A hydraulic spreading tool can pry the door open.

MATCH THE WORDS TO THE PICTURES!

The answers are on the bottom of the page.

1. rescue tools

a.

2. fire engine

b.

3. fire hose

c.

4. turnout gear

d.

TEST YOUR TOOL KNOWLEDGE!

The answers are on the bottom of the page.

1.

Turnout gear is able to **withstand** 5000-degree heat.

TRUE OR FALSE?

2.

Some fire engines can hold up to 3,000 **gallons** of water.

TRUE OR FALSE?

3.

Fire hoses can only be held by one person at a time.

TRUE OR FALSE?

4.

Hydraulic rescue tools can both cut and spread.

TRUE OR FALSE?

TOOL QUIZ

Answers: 1) false 2) true 3) false 4) true

GLOSSARY

attached – joined or connected.

dangerous – able or likely to cause harm or injury.

equipment – a set of tools or items used for a special purpose or activity.

fabric – woven material or cloth.

gallon – a unit for measuring liquids. Milk and gasoline are often sold by the gallon.

hydraulic – operated by the pressure of liquid being forced through a small hole or tube.

nozzle – a short tube on the end of a hose or pipe that controls the flow of liquid.

siren – a device that makes a loud sound as a signal or warning.

suppress – to make something stop.

withstand – to survive or resist the effect of something.